AROUND THE WORLD

Leon

Hetty

Professor
Verne

Brigit

Toosant

Newton

Headway · Hodder & Stoughton

In the nineteenth century Jules Verne, the famous author, wrote exciting books about journeys of adventure. Now his namesake, Professor Bartholemew Verne, has invented an amazing machine. In it he can follow the journeys Jules Verne wrote about. With his crew of children, he can explore the wonders of the world and of outer space.

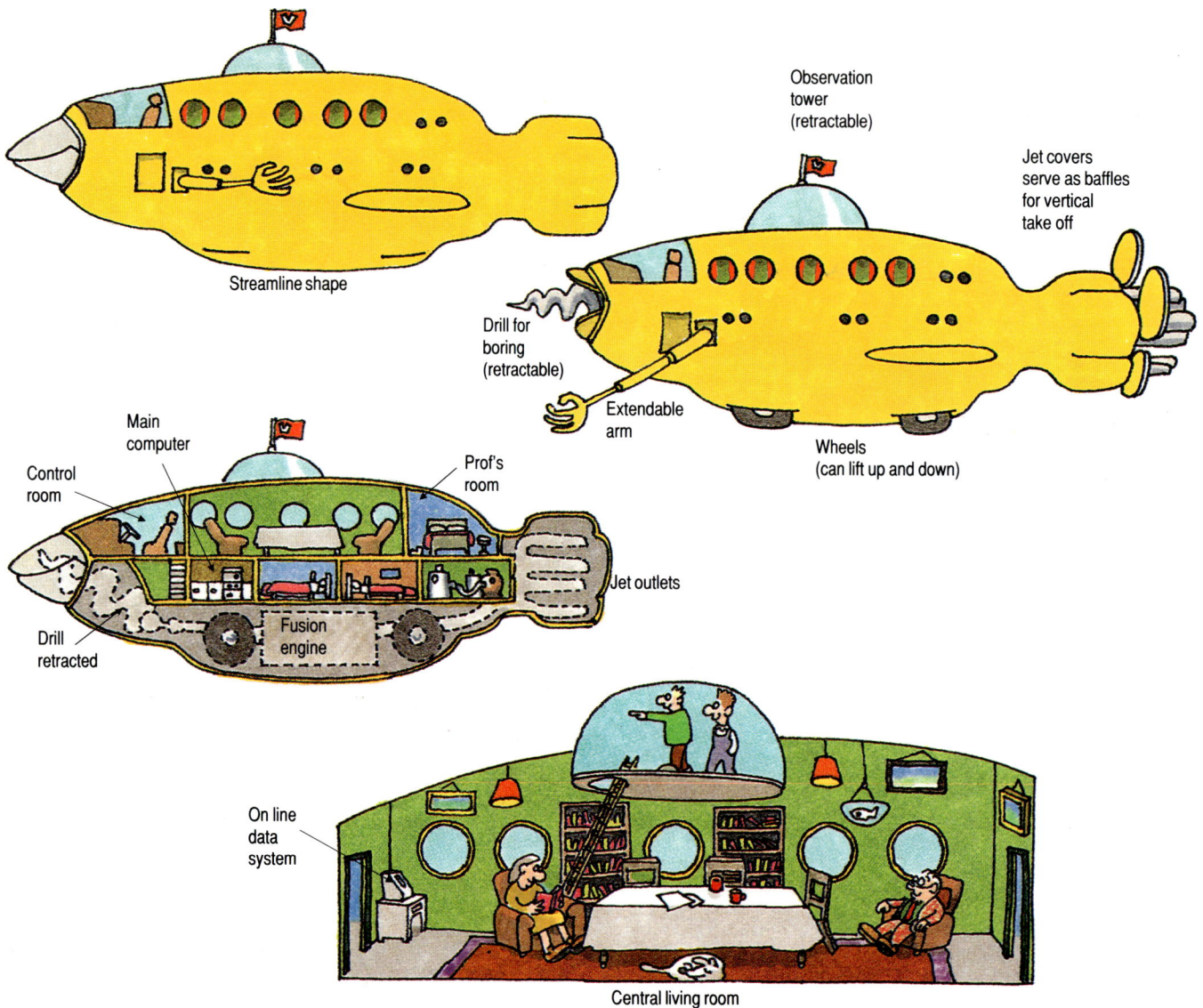

Streamline shape

Observation tower (retractable)

Jet covers serve as baffles for vertical take off

Drill for boring (retractable)

Extendable arm

Wheels (can lift up and down)

Main computer

Control room

Prof's room

Drill retracted

Fusion engine

Jet outlets

On line data system

Central living room

In 1873 Jules Verne wrote a book called AROUND THE WORLD IN EIGHTY DAYS. In the book, a man had to travel around the whole world in eighty days or less in order to win a bet.

Did he manage it?

Yes he did.

Now we are going to go around the world.

Wow!

Great!

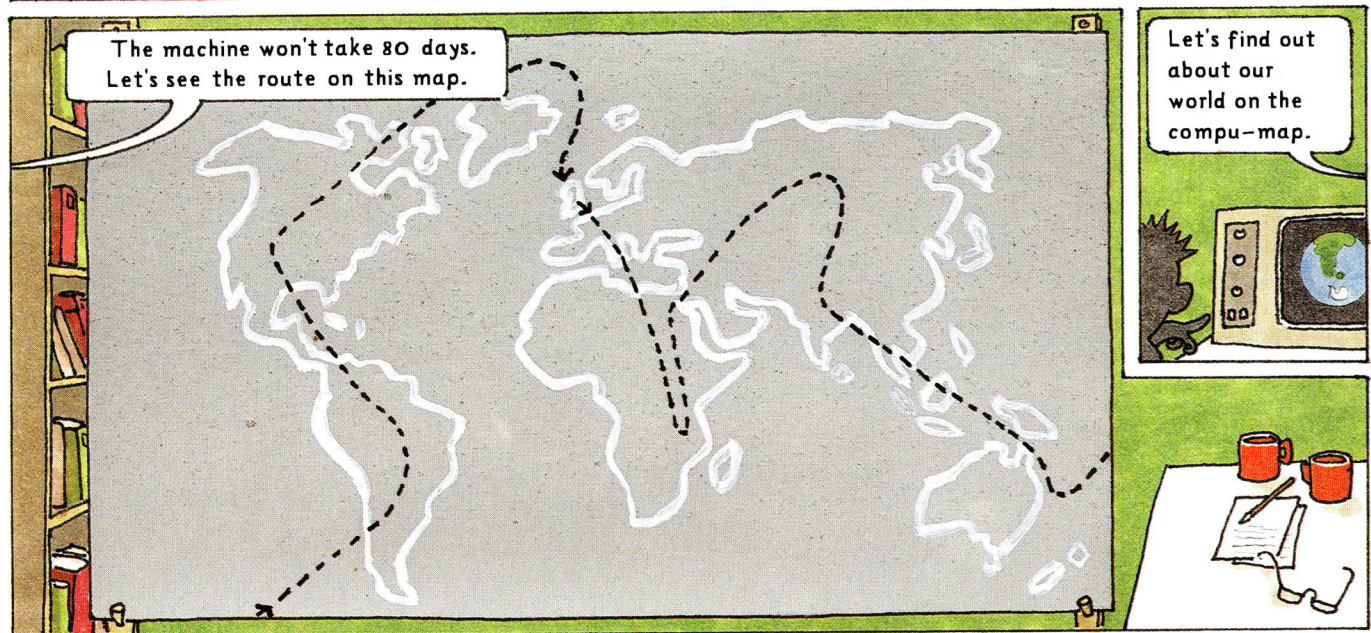

The machine won't take 80 days. Let's see the route on this map.

Let's find out about our world on the compu-map.

COMPU-MAP
The Earth is not a perfect sphere.

Size: 38,165 km around the equator
36,357 km around the poles
12,714 km polar diameter
12,756 km equatorial diameter

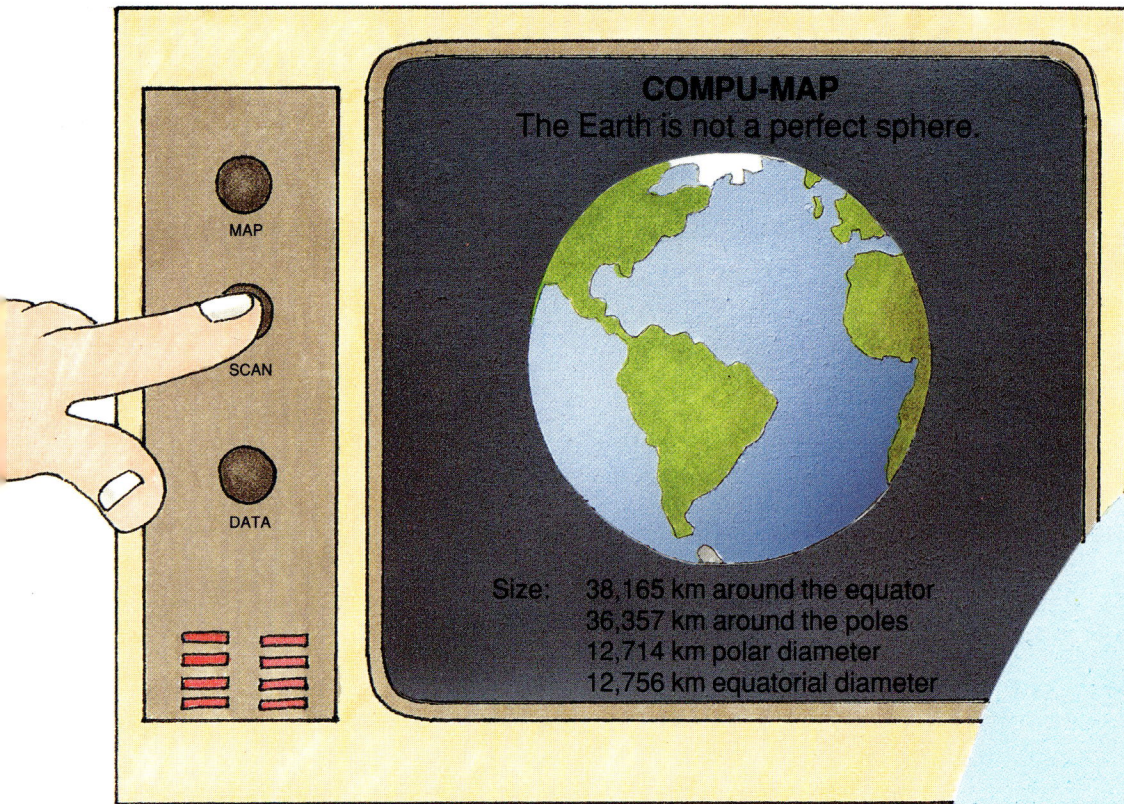

Right! Let's find out more about our world on the compu-map.

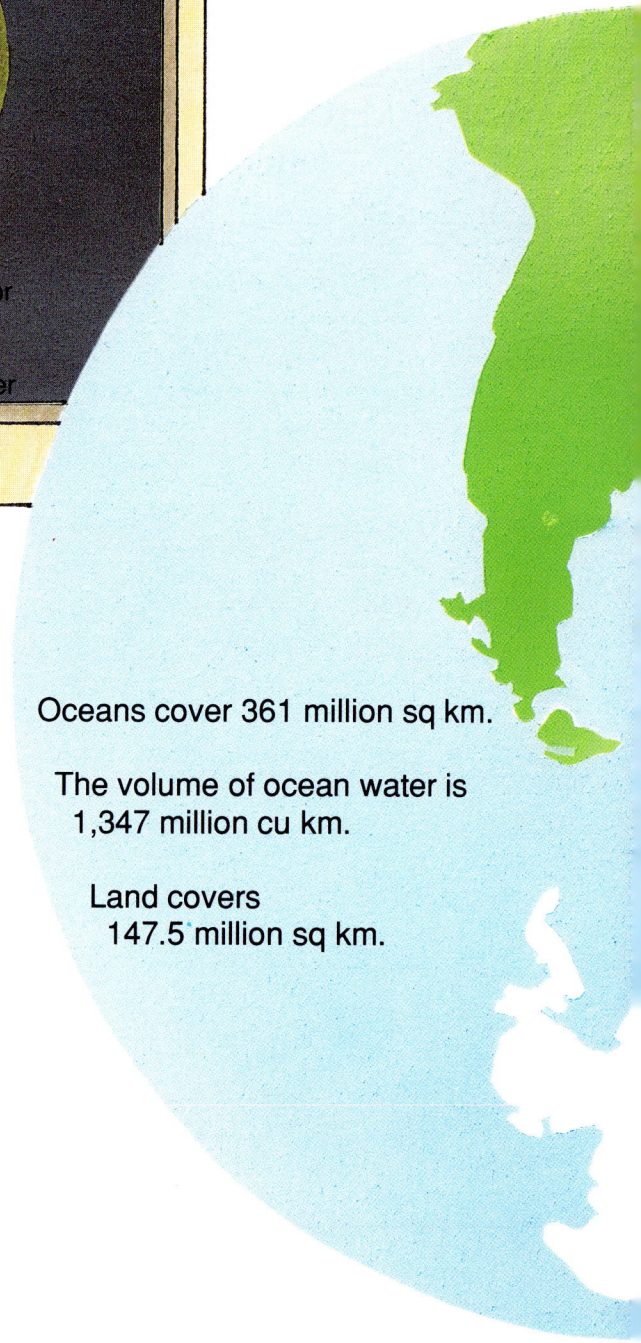

MAP

SCAN

DATA

COMPU-DATA

Estimated to be 4,600 million years old. The Earth was probably formed at the same time as the Sun. Seventy-one percent of the world is covered by water.

Oceans cover 361 million sq km.

The volume of ocean water is 1,347 million cu km.

Land covers 147.5 million sq km.

COMPU-DATA

The world's population is about 5,000 million. It is growing by a quarter of a million every day!
Fifty-eight percent of the world's population lives in Asia.

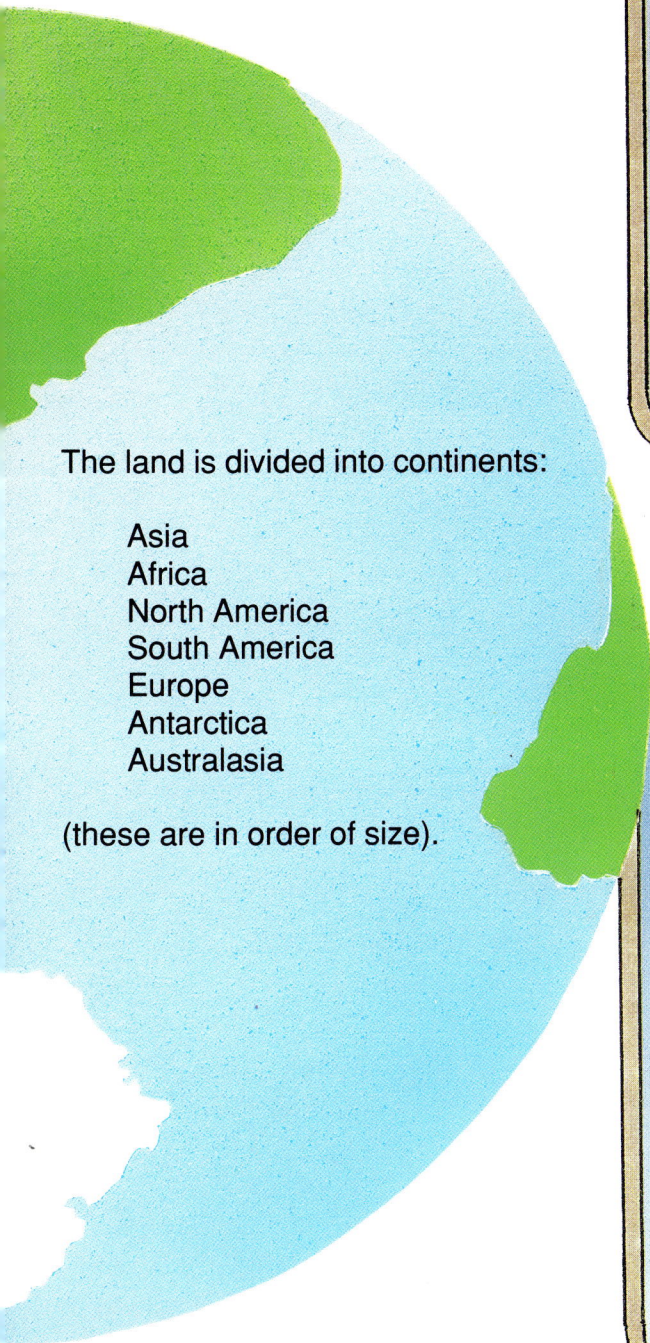

The land is divided into continents:

Asia
Africa
North America
South America
Europe
Antarctica
Australasia

(these are in order of size).

COMPU-DATA

Climate is the word used to describe the usual weather and temperature found in an area.

The climate of a particular place is affected by:

1. How far north or south of the equator it is. The further from the equator, the colder the climate.
2. How close it is to the sea. The nearer to the coast, the less extreme the climate.
3. How high it is above sea level. The higher it is, the colder the climate.

The same types of climates are found in different parts of the world. For instance, rain forests can be found in Africa, South America and Asia.

COMPU-DATA

MAP

SCAN

DATA

Warning!
Bison are protected by law.

What a great view!

It's the temperate region.

Lovely!

So green!

COMPU-MAP

The temperate regions of the world

Most of Northern Europe and North America are in the temperate region. This means that the climate is never very hot or very cold. There is also an ideal amount of rainfall for plants and trees to grow. Hundreds of years ago much of Europe was covered in forests. Most of these have now been cut down by people to make space for fields and towns. These forests were once the home of many animals such as wolves, bears, deer and bison. The destruction of the forests has meant that these animals lost their homes and their numbers fell. Nowadays, animals like bison are protected by law.

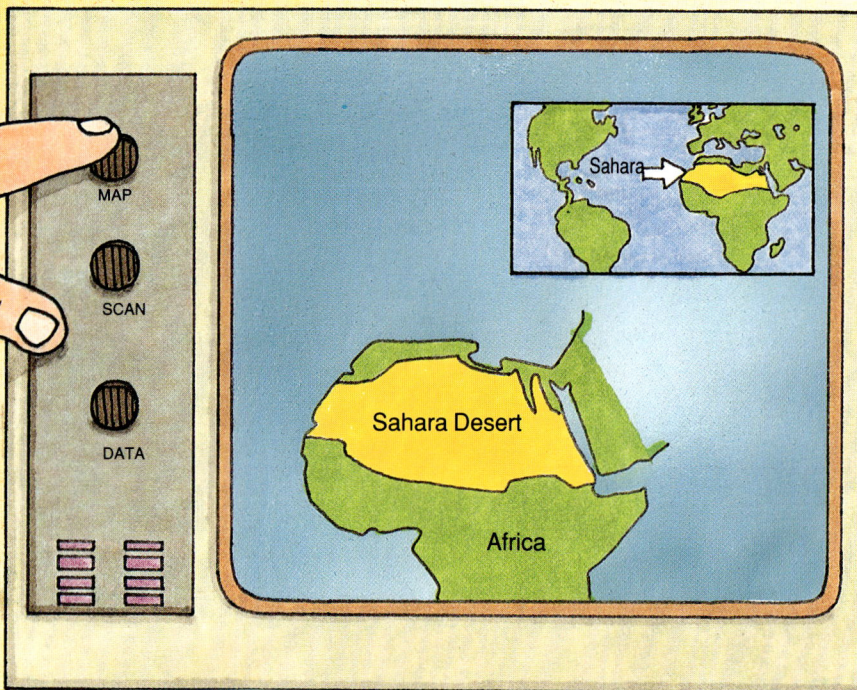

Fifteen thousand years ago, the Sahara was a fertile area, with rivers, trees and grasslands. Then the climate changed and the hotter winds caused the streams to dry up. This in turn caused the land to dry up and the soil to break down. Today, the Sahara is the world's largest desert.

8

Many people think that deserts are made up of just sand. This is wrong. Areas of sand, called *ergs*, cover only fifteen percent of the Sahara. Seventy percent of the Sahara desert is made up of stone plateaus (hammada) and gravel (reg). There are also three mountains – the Ahagger, Tibesti and Aïr. These rise up to more than 3,350 m (11,000 feet) high.

Because there is very little rain, there is little animal and plant life. Those animals that do survive in the Sahara can go without water for long periods. Lizards, snakes and gerbils (desert rats) live in the desert. They hunt for food at night when it is cooler.

SANDSTORMS

Incredible sandstorms happen in the Sahara. The wind can blow at up to 48 km per hour (30 miles per hour) and create sandstorms 1.6 km (1 mile) high and up to 480 km (300 miles) wide!

COMPU-MAP

Ethiopia

Kenya

Serengeti Park

AP

SCAN

DATA

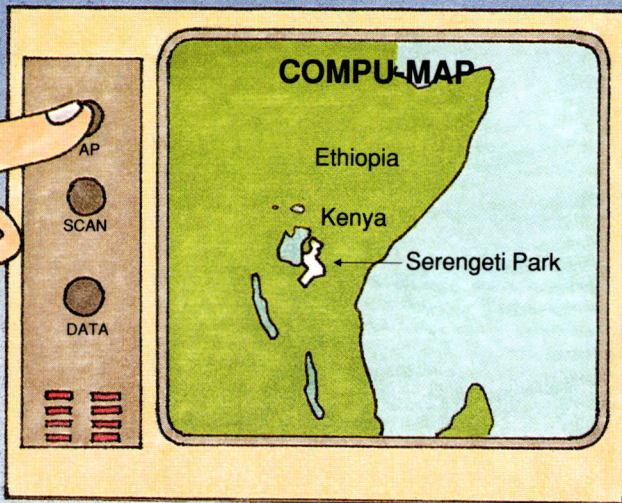

The Serengeti National Park is situated
in the heart of Africa's grasslands.
Grasslands are spread all over the world.
The grasslands which grow in tropical
areas are called *Savannas*. The climate is
always hot, but there are two seasons:
a wet one followed by a dry one.

Tall grasses and low trees grow in the Savanna and it
is home to millions of grass-eating animals (herbivores),
such as antelopes, wildebeest, elephants, giraffes,
rhinoceroses and zebras. These animals in turn
provide food for meat-eating animals (carnivores),
such as lions, cheetahs, leopards and hyenas.

In the Serengeti National Park animals are protected from hunting. However,
there is a problem from poachers who kill animals for their skin, horns or tusks.

Area: **14,800 sq km**
(**5,700 sq miles**)

Founded: **1941**

COMPU-DATA

The Great Rift Valley cuts through the Serengeti National Park. It is the longest crack in the Earth's surface. It is 8,700 km long and stretches from Syria all the way to Mozambique!

Cor! That's fast!

Yes, 100 km per hour!

Camera shots are the only shots allowed.

Thank goodness!

River Nile

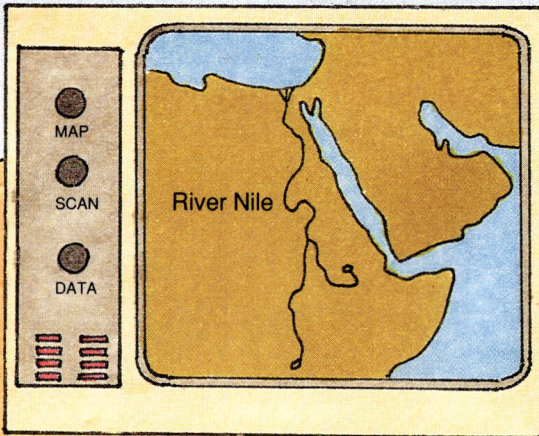

The River Nile is made up of two rivers: the Blue Nile and the White Nile. The Blue Nile begins in Lake Tana, Ethiopia and runs for 1,610 km. The White Nile is 3,700 km long. Its source is the Luvironza River in Burundi. The two rivers join together at Khartoum in Sudan, before flowing across Egypt and into the Mediterranean Sea.

Nearly a tenth of Africa is dependant to some extent on the Nile. Its waters provide irrigation for agriculture and hydro-electric power. The river has been used as a means of transport for thousands of years.

The Nile Crocodile is the most ferocious species of crocodile in the world. It attacks animals that come to drink, and drags them under the surface of the water. It is also called a man-killer, because it has killed so many humans.

COMPU-DATA

Pyramids were built as tombs for Pharaohs (Egyptian kings) nearly 4,000 years ago! The Great Pyramid of Cheops at Giza is made up of over two million stone blocks.

Don't get too close!

Smile please!

Is this all right?

Nearly half of Siberia is covered by a huge band of forest called *Taiga*. This is a Russian word meaning 'cold forest'. Only coniferous trees such as spruce, pine and fir can survive in the cold Siberian climate. These types of trees are also known as evergreens because they keep their leaves all year round, unlike deciduous trees which lose their leaves in winter.

The Siberian forest is vast, stretching nearly the whole length of Siberia and measuring up to 2,000 km wide.

Because of the harsh climatic conditions, very few humans live in this area. However, the Taiga is the perfect home for bears and wolves and these roam the cold, dark forests hunting for food.

The trees from this region are very important for the timber and paper-making trades. Millions are cut down every year. There are also valuable minerals to be found in the northern forests. Gold, copper and uranium are mined, and oil has been found in Western Siberia.

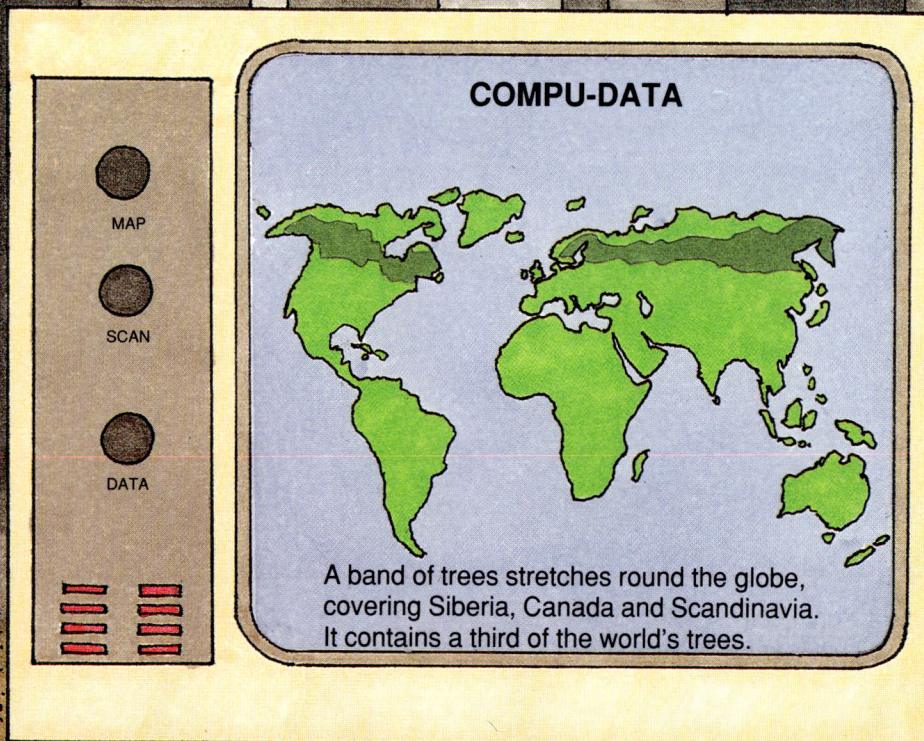

COMPU-DATA

A band of trees stretches round the globe, covering Siberia, Canada and Scandinavia. It contains a third of the world's trees.

MAP

SCAN

DATA

14

Size: **3 million sq km** (1.87 million sq miles)

Temperature: **Winter: as low as -45°C (-49°F)** **Summer: as high as 20°C (68°F)**

16

Mount Everest is the highest mountain in the world. It stands on the border of Tibet and Nepal in the Himalayan mountain range. The Himalayas extend for 2,410 km (1,500 miles) through Pakistan, India, Tibet, Nepal, Sikkim and Bhutan. They contain several of the world's highest mountains.

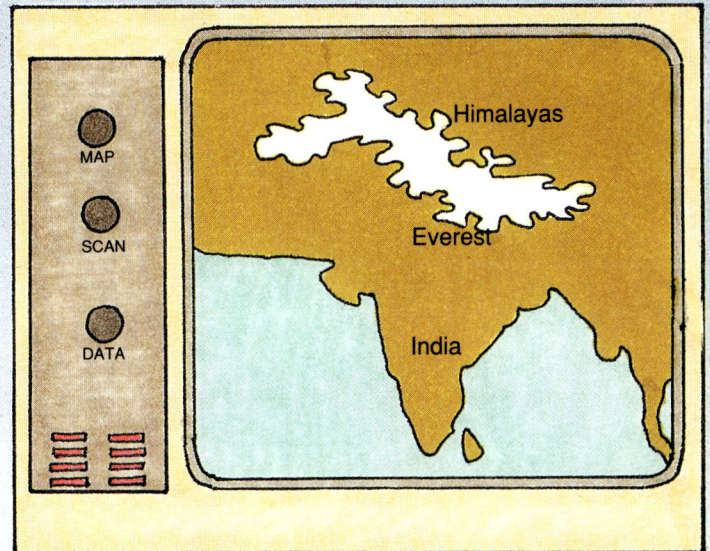

The Himalayas began to be formed over 60 million years ago when two of the Earth's huge moving plates of rock, called *tectonic plates*, crashed into each other. The land broke, folded and buckled. Over a period of millions of years this land was lifted up and created the huge mountain range. This lifting has not yet stopped – it is estimated that the Himalayas are growing at a rate of 5 cm a year!

The people of Tibet and Nepal call Everest 'Chomolungma', which means 'Goddess-mother of the Earth'.

COMPU-DATA

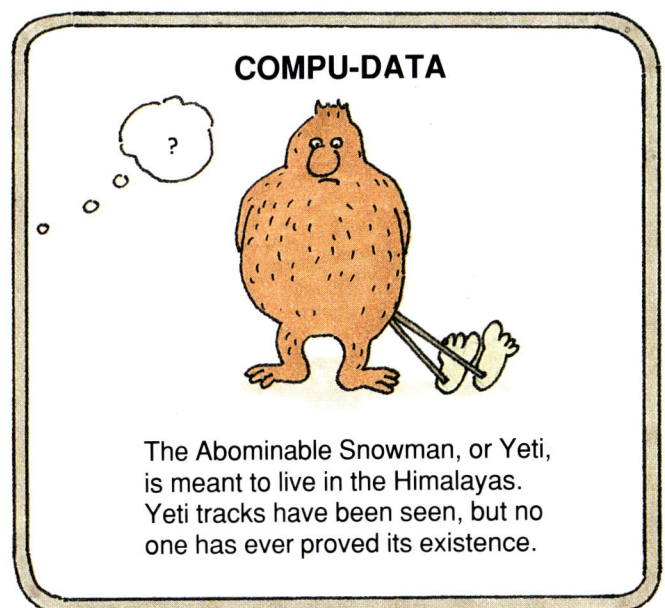

The Abominable Snowman, or Yeti, is meant to live in the Himalayas. Yeti tracks have been seen, but no one has ever proved its existence.

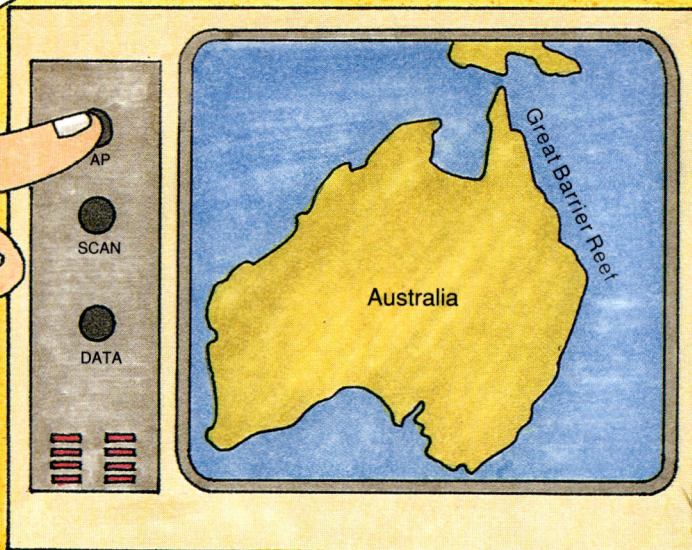

AP

SCAN

DATA

Australia

Great Barrier Reef

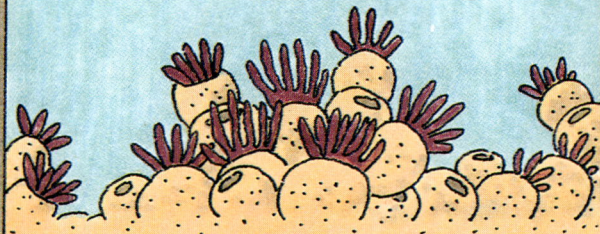

COMPU-DATA

Corals have limestone skeletons. As old corals die, new ones grow on top, and after thousands of years, huge piles of corals form called reefs. The Great Barrier Reef is made up of over 350 different coral species.

It's lovely and warm!

Don't touch the coral. It can be delicate.

| Size: **259,000 sq km** | Length: **2,010 km** | Width: **Up to 122 m** |
| **(100,000 sq miles)** | **(1,250 miles)** | **(400 feet)** |

The Great Barrier Reef is the largest coral reef in the world. It is separated from the mainland of Australia by a shallow lagoon up to 161 km (100 miles) wide. The reef is the greatest structure made by any living thing on the Earth. It is made by millions of tiny animals called corals.

These corals have formed thousands of individual reefs, gardens and islets. In some places the reef is 122 m (400 feet) thick. The Great Barrier Reef is home to over 1,400 different species of fish. Unusual marine life such as sponges, sea urchins, sea cucumbers and star fish also live in the reef.

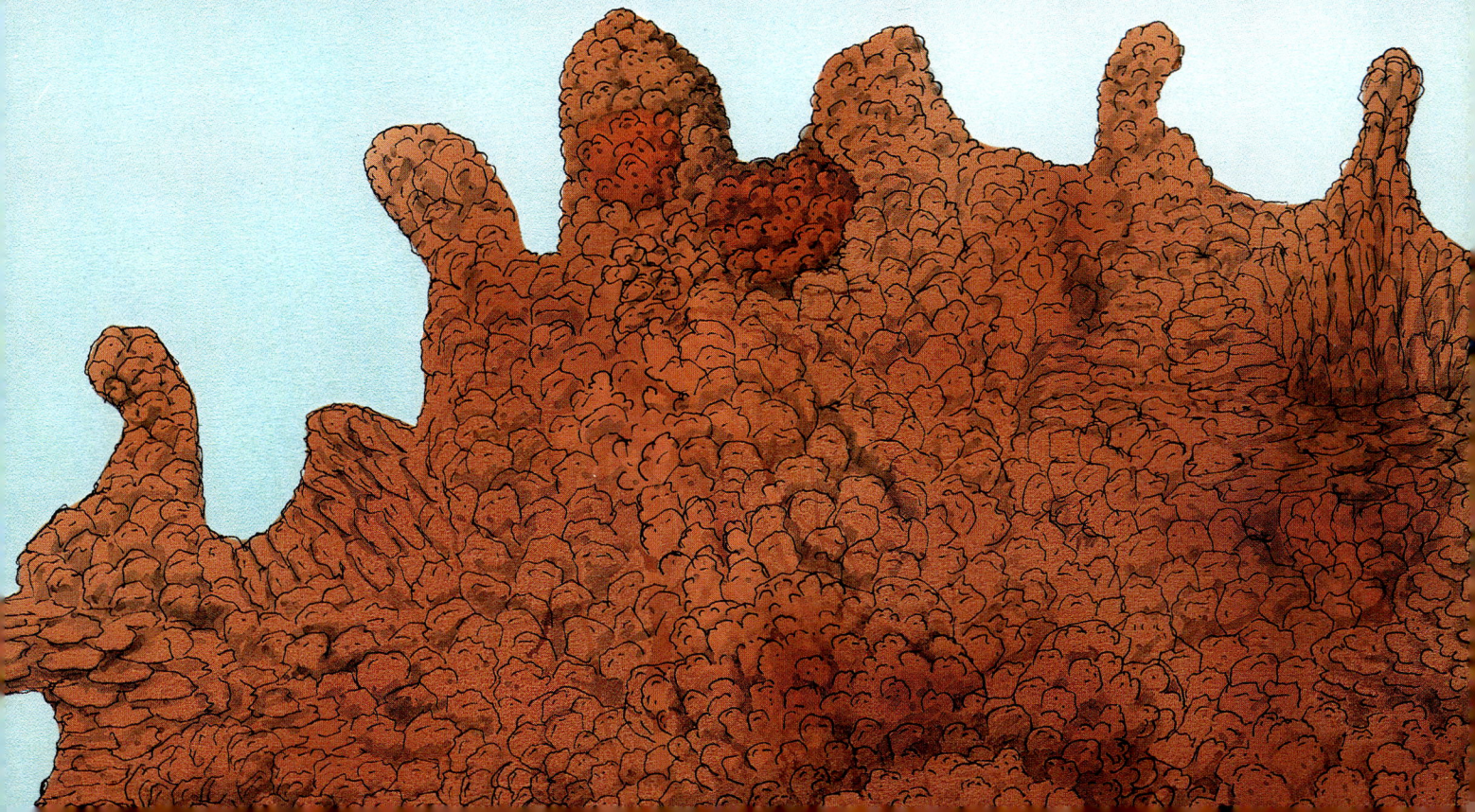

Seen many dogfish?

Just think, there's nothing but water for *11,033* m below me!

That's what they think!

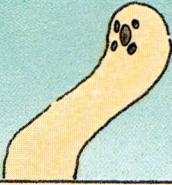

AP

SCAN

DATA

Pacific
Ocean

**Size: 181.3 million sq km
(70 million sq miles)**

**Deepest point: The Challenger Deep in the Marianas Trench –
11,033 m (36,198 feet) deep**

Volcanic island

COMPU-DATA

The Pacific Ocean is being ruined by the activities of man. The water is being polluted and too many fish are being caught. Some of the fishing ships in the Pacific trail nets up to 100 km long. These catch lots of fish, but also trap and kill sea birds, whales and dolphins.

There are five oceans covering the Earth. These are the Atlantic, Arctic, the Indian, the Southern (or Antarctic) and the Pacific. The Pacific Ocean is the world's largest and deepest ocean. It stretches from the Arctic to the Antarctic and from North and South America to Asia and Australia.

The Pacific covers about a third of the Earth's surface. There are approximately 20,000 islands in the Pacific. The islands that ring the Pacific are volcanic and are know as the *Circum-Pacific Ring of Fire.*

The islands are the home of many species of plants and animals that are not found anywhere else in the world.

Size: **14,245,000 sq km**
(5,500,000 sq miles)

Temperature: Average in winter (June): -57°C (-70°F)
Average in summer (January): -18°C (0°F)

Antarctica is the coldest place on Earth. Winds can blow up to 320 km per hour, and temperatures can reach as low as -88°C. The only life in Antarctica is in or near the sea. Penguins, seabirds and seals surround the Antarctic coastline. The sea is rich in krill, a small shrimp-like creature. This is the main diet of the fish and whales of these Antarctic waters.

Twenty-five million years ago, Antarctica was covered with trees and grass. Then the temperature grew colder and the land became covered with ice and snow. Ninety percent of the world's ice is in Antarctica. In some places it is nearly 5 km deep. If all this ice melted, the Earth's water levels would rise by 60 m.

Beneath the ice are valuable minerals like coal, iron, lead and copper. Some people believe there is oil. But mining for these would destroy Antarctica and its wildlife.

COMPU-DATA

The male Emperor Penguin balances the egg on his feet and covers it with a layer of skin. This keeps it warm until it hatches out two months later.

I see why it's called a rain forest.

Atlantic Ocean

Equator

Amazon rain forest

South America

AP

SCAN

DATA

Tropical rain forests are also known as *equatorial forests*. This is because they are scattered over the world in a band across the equator.

The Amazon rain forest is the largest rain forest in the world. It surrounds the River Amazon, which at 6,437 km (4,000 miles) long, is the second longest river in the world.

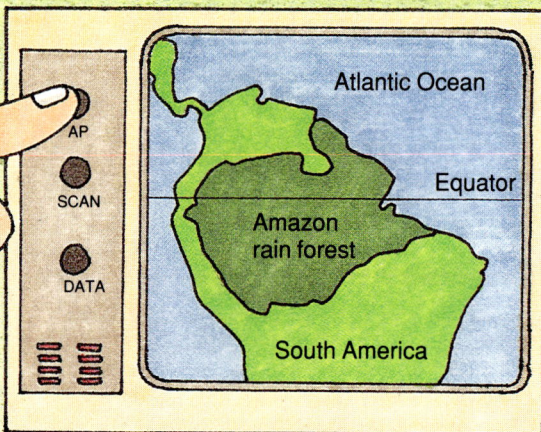

Average temperature: **27° to 28°C**
(80° to 82°F)

Annual rainfall: **181 cm**
(71 inches)

Conditions: **Hot and**
wet all year

Wow, umbrellicus insecticus
– very rare!

How?

What?

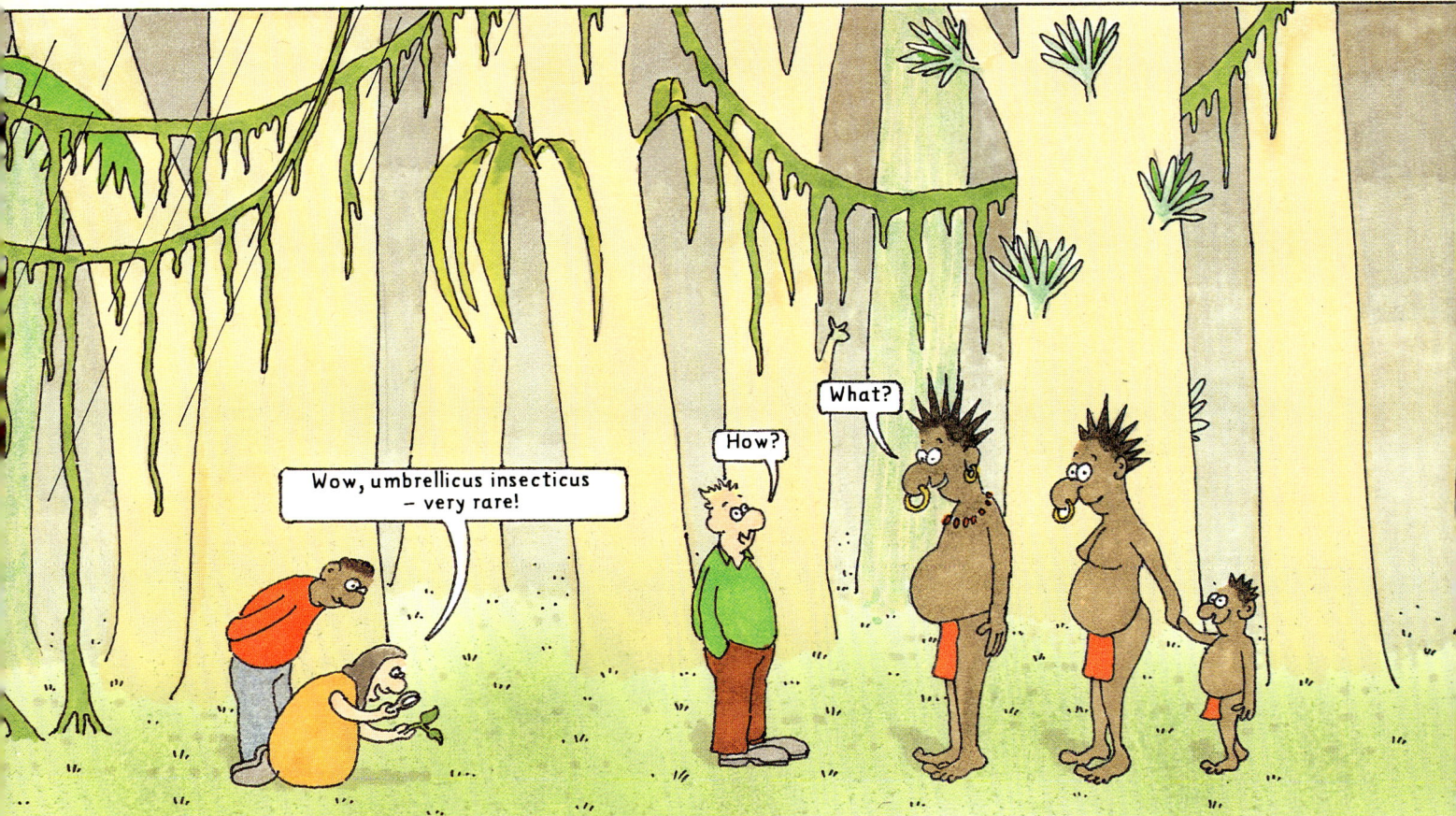

Rain forests are very important – they help to control the world's climate and they are also home to millions of species of animals and plants. Many of these plants are used to make medicines. But large areas of rain forest are being cut down. It is estimated that one acre of rain forest is being destroyed EVERY SECOND! If this continues, the Amazon rain forest will not exist in thirty years, and the animals and plants of the forest will be gone for ever.

COMPU-DATA

Carbon
dioxide

Oxygen

Rain forests help control the world's climate. Leaves change carbon dioxide into oxygen. We breathe oxygen. Less trees means less oxygen and more carbon dioxide.

USA

Grand
Canyon

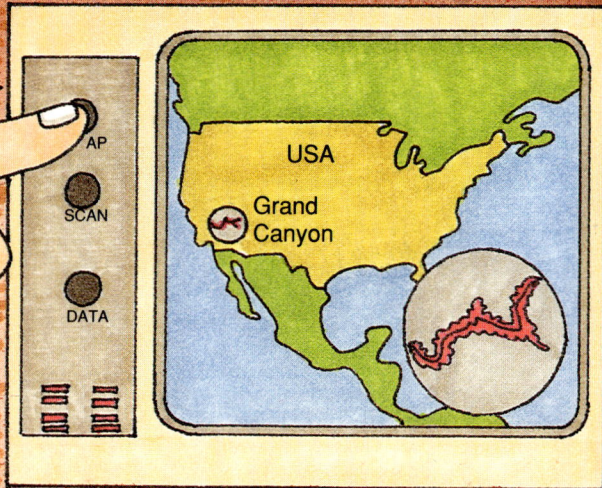

The Grand Canyon is the world's largest gorge. Its walls have been created by the waters of the River Colorado which flow through the gorge. Over a period of 8 million years, the water has worn away the rocks and made the gorge deeper and deeper. This erosion has revealed many different layers of rock. By studying these, scientists have been able to gain more information about the history of the Earth.

COMPU-DATA

TO THE CANYON

In prehistoric times, tribes of Pueblo Indians made their home in the gorge. They dug out caves in the lower walls of the canyon and lived in these. Indian tribes live in the surrounding areas today.

The rocks at the top of the gorge are about 250 million years old and consist of sandstones, shales and limestones. The rocks at Granite Gorge, the deepest point of the canyon, are volcanic and thought to be over 2,000 million years old. The sides are so steep tourists travel down to the bottom on mules.

Length: **349.2 km**
(217 miles)

Width: **6.4 to 29 km**
(4 to 18 miles)

Depth: **1.6 km (1 mile)**
at Granite Gorge

Destination: **THE ARCTIC**

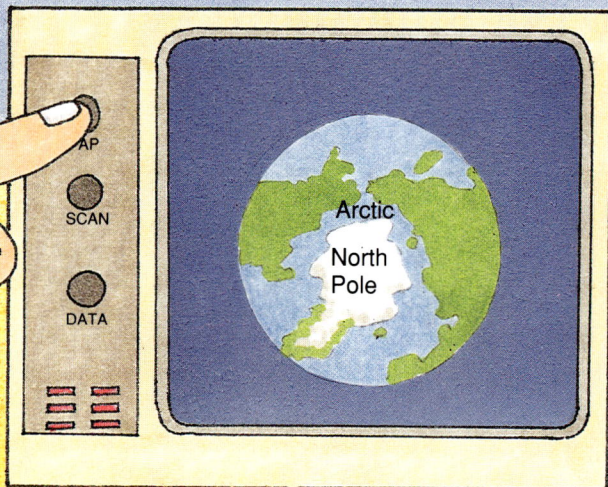

The Arctic is at the very top of the Earth. It consists of all the land and sea inside an imaginary line that circles the Earth. This is called the *Arctic Circle*. In this area, the winters are long and cold and the summers are short and cool.

The Arctic Ocean, (the world's smallest ocean), is permanently frozen. Unlike the South Pole, there is no land at the North Pole, only ice.

Arctic

North Pole

AP

SCAN

DATA

That's a Musk Ox!

Its coat is thicker than yours, Prof.

28

The gently sloping lands that surround the Arctic Ocean are called *Tundra*. No trees grow in the Tundra because the ground just below the surface is always frozen rock hard. This is called *permafrost*.

Plant life consists of shrubs and lichens. These are the main food of several kinds of animal, including Caribou (tamed Caribou are called Reindeer), and Musk Oxen.

Polar bears also eat plants, but their main diet is fish and seals. Only a few birds live in the Tundra all the year round, but in the summer hundreds of birds migrate there to breed.

The native humans that live in the Polar and Tundra regions are the Inuits (or Eskimos) in North America, and the Sami (or Lapps) in north Scandinavia.

Ug!

COMPU-DATA

Another cup?

Where's the sugar?

In the middle of summer in the Arctic circle, the sun never sets. That's why it's called the land of the midnight sun. But in the winter there are days when the sun never rises and the land is in permanent darkness.

COMPU-DATA

International Date Line.

> Hey! That calendar's wrong! It says today is the 12th, but my digital watch says it's the 13th.

> We travelled eastwards, so we had two Mondays. That's why your watch is wrong. You didn't reset it.

The world is divided into different time zones. This is done to make time correspond with day and night. Noon should be in the middle of daylight, and midnight in the middle of darkness all over the world. So, if it is noon in Britain, it is 10.00 p.m. in Sidney, Australia, and 7.00 a.m. in New York, USA.

Halfway round the world, there is an imaginary line down the 180 degrees meridian of longitude. This is called the *International Date Line*. If you cross it the date changes! If you are travelling westwards you add a day, if you are travelling eastwards you subtract a day from your journey.

So if you travel west on a Sunday at one minute to midnight and cross the date line, it becomes one minute past midnight on Tuesday morning! If you travel east on a Monday at one minute to midnight and cross the date line, it becomes one minute past midnight on Monday again.

Crossing the International Date Line

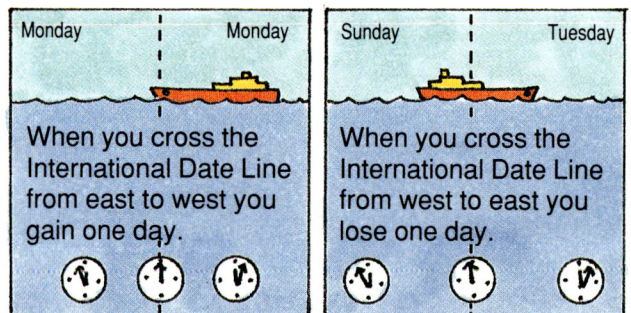

Monday	Monday	Sunday	Tuesday
When you cross the International Date Line from east to west you gain one day.		When you cross the International Date Line from west to east you lose one day.	

Now try my quiz, to see how much you can remember about the world.

Professor Verne's *Around the World* **quiz**

1. ***Where is the coldest place on Earth?***
   a) your refrigerator
   b) the Arctic
   c) Antarctica

2. ***What does the word 'Taiga' mean?***
   a) striped animal
   b) cold forest
   c) dark place

3. ***Which is the longest river in the world?***
   a) the Amazon
   b) the Nile
   c) the Thames

4. ***How often is an acre of rain forest being destroyed?***
   a) every 100 years
   b) every second
   c) every time it rains

5. ***Which is the highest mountain in the world?***
   a) Mount Everest
   b) Mount Ain
   c) Mount Never-rest

6. ***Which river flows through the Grand Canyon?***
   a) the Colorado
   b) the Nile
   c) the Amazon

Answers: 1) c.   2) b.   3) b.   4) b.   5) a.   6) a.

INDEX

British Library Cataloguing in Publication Data
Skidmore, Steve
  Around the World. - (Fantastic Journey Series)
  I. Title II. Series
  910.4
ISBN 0 340 57080 6
First published 1992
© 1992 Steve Skidmore/Lazy Summer Books

Printed in Great Britain for the educational publishing division of Hodder and Stoughton Ltd, Mill Road, Dunton Green, Sevenoaks, Kent by Cambus Litho Limited, East Kilbride.